Roberta
and other poems

also by Ricardo Quinones

North/South: The Great European Divide
(U Toronto P 2016)

Fringes
(39 West Press 2015)

Finishing Touches
(39 West Press 2014)

A Sorting of the Ways: New and Selected Poems
(39 West Press 2011)

Through the Years
(39 West Press 2010)

Erasmus and Voltaire: Why They Still Matter
(U Toronto P 2010)

Dualisms: The Agons of the Modern World
(U Toronto P 2007)

Foundation Sacrifice in Dante's "Commedia"
(Penn State UP 1994)

The Changes of Cain: Violence and the Lost Brother
(Princeton UP 1991)

Mapping Literary Modernism: Time and Development
(Princeton UP 1985)

Dante Alighieri
(Twayne 1979; updated revised edition 1998)

The Renaissance Discovery of Time
(Harvard UP 1972)

Roberta
and other poems

Ricardo Quinones

39 WEST PRESS
Kansas City, MO
www.39WestPress.com

Copyright © 2011 by Ricardo Quinones

All rights reserved. No part of this book may be reproduced, scanned, or distributed in any printed or electronic form, including information storage and retrieval systems, without permission. Please do not participate in or encourage piracy of copyrighted materials in violation of the author's rights. Please purchase only authorized editions.

First Edition: March 2011

ISBN: 978-0-615-46249-3

This book is a work of fiction. Names, characters, places, dates, and incidents are products of the author's imagination, or are used fictitiously, satirically, or as parody. Any resemblance to actual persons, living or dead, business establishments, events, or locales is entirely coincidental.

10 9 8 7 6 5 4 3 2

Design & Layout: j.d.tulloch
Front Cover Painting: Herbstsonne und Bäume (1912) by Egon Schiele

39WP-03A

CONTENTS

PART ONE: ROBERTA

Odalisque	3
For Roberta on Her Birthday	4
Delight and Reserve	6
February 15: Roberta's Day	8
R & R: Valentine's Day III	10
Tuesdays	12

PART TWO: OTHER POEMS

Rocks and Their Fellow Travelers	17
Wallet Poems IV	23
Dispatched	26
Profanities	28

Part One
Roberta

Odalisque

A man might be transformed
But a woman is transfigured
By the gracious beauties of love's intent.
When spread to its full extent
Her body is like majesty unfurled
Her composure is so confidently contained
That beyond her figure there is no world.
She is gifted to the heights of splendor
There is nothing she does not own
Even birds hover in flight
Unwilling to relinquish their place in the light.
Her breath emanates through her pores
Not a particule is ignored;
Her hair when fanned is strewn like willows
And when she stretches
It's as if the world set sail
A picture of grace in a field of motion.
Pleasure abounds at each recommencement
Making it more like a constant flow
An equipoise of undiluted bliss
A sheen of gossamer covers her glow
A Greenwich of time is centered here
From which all things start and go.

From the beginning this was the world's way
Despite what other books might say
A modulated pace of sheer delight
No womb and tomb or death and Eros
Not even Cleopatra burning bright
But a human measure that embodies life
Giving a grounding to the paths of light.
First founded in woman's delight.

For Roberta on Her Birthday

There is a loving beyond love
That doesn't come from below or above
But keeps a constant human sphere
A staunchness of character
A loyalty that adheres
Which gathering through the years
Was not quite understood when we held hands
And together swore those bands.

The reigns of time, biology and history
Certainly have exacted their tolls.
We too were young and foolish
Pushing blindly with the pedal
When the brake worked just as well
Our miscarriages were blatant
Excused only by our need to know
What was urging us through the snow.

And snow it did and does now
As we watch through the window
The magic of wintertime's sun
Our age has slowed us down
The fierce virility a thing long done
But that does not mean we are gliding
Staunchness of character
And loyalty through distress
Are not passive virtues and have no rest,
Constantly put to the test
By the Nietzschean Uber-mensch
Or the will to power
We know what wisdom has taught
Ours are the lessons experience has wrought
That down through years deliver the trust
The metals that will not rust
A rightness of kind worked by benevolence of mind.

And as we enter the fog of the night
Not much shall remain
Our hands shall crumble
Flat stones shall plane our earth
Our names inscribed thereon
And other fruitless data of years
But not the realities that they meant
Of two people joined by their trusting intent.

Delight and Reserve

Innocence is delightful
But Delight in all its movings
Has an innocence as well.
Delight is totally engaged
And that rarely can go wrong.
Delight that poor man's folly is whole,
Seeking no other support
Nor other minding to bear,
No searchings elsewhere.
Self-sufficing, self-sustained
Attaining in moments direct
An ascendency not had by power:
We delight in another's delight.
Why priests and gods can do no other
But bless a woman in throes of pleasure.

There is in Reserve an earnest
Not meant for display.
Must all the push be red on black
Florid beyond measure,
With nothing held back
Arms flaying needfully
Over-wrought and beyond contact?
Autumn's colors are fetching, too—
Abundance in Reserve
A mine of memory adhering.
Reserve's still water is private
And its holdings stately,
Correct and never failing speech
Nothing beyond our reach,
Why priests and gods regard as blest
A woman collected, in herself possessed.

They fare different weather
Delight and Reserve, Reserve and Delight
Sisters of bright provenance
Like silver streams from pictured vases
Replenishing our earthly stations
Each making the other better.
Reserve without Delight
Would have no place to go;
Delight without Reserve
Would loosen all in show.

Roberta, my love, they pour in you
Those streamings of lordly treasure
Those beckonings of marital pleasure
If only I can meet them to your measure.

February 15: Roberta's Day*

The pronunciation of your day
Requires no saints to adorn your name.
Come from the Foxes and the Roses
California's bushes and briars
Small farms and horses
That weather your sun-fed ways.

Although no saints abound
This date is honor's stall of renown
More prominent by omen
Of secular saints who work our weal
Impressing as in a seal
Three crowns that meet
To herald your future sway.

It is Susan B. Anthony's day
An abolitionist spurned
Who Christian Temperance turned
Into a Woman's Union
A sisterhood of gentler base
Thus bringing gender to nation and race.

On this date the Maine went under
And capsized too the Empire of Spain
But up there arose the American fleet
And the Spanish generation of '98
Whose cross-fires you came to arbitrate.

Theses two crowns need a third,
But not quite yet.
This date is Lupercalia
Famed for its boisterous fetes
When young athletes of bodily sheen
Raced through the narrow Roman streets
Like running of bulls in Spain
Fertility was all the hunt
Not a single string of goatish sheen
But with maleness swinging free
Whipping the matrons to a frenzied glee
And a fervor to their stomping feet.

On this date another Anthony
That glorious runner and generous friend
Tempted Caesar with the diadem
Whose leafy coverlet and verge
Provides the august shade
That guards the face
Against those loathsome sprites
Those demons of the sun-lit sky
That pierce and dig more harm
Than all the armies of the night.

So we invoke what birth intended
As signs and figures, forerunners along the way
To be emblazoned on this day.
To the protection of these crowns
We only add this parasol of care
That no harm come to your gentle skin
As you continue to front the winds
And the malevolent powers of the air.

On her father's side, Roberta came from the family of Fox, and on her mother's, from the family of Rose. One of her prominent studies was <u>Gender and Nation in the Spanish Modernist Novel</u>, which was preceded by <u>Crossfire: Philosophy in the Novel in Spain 1900-1934</u>. She periodically has to be treated for spots of skin cancer, and she was given a parasol on her birthday.

R & R: Valentine's Day III

Still striving in our third year.
Did I say third
When I meant thirteenth, my dear.
Such computations, however veiled,
Cannot begin to rescind or even restrain
The rampant tinglings of desire;
Nor can temperance or illness deter
The ardors of this third or thirteenth year.

Is sex the last frontier?
That can hardly be.
Since it certainly was the first.
But it does keep to task
That good garden start
Which neither gods nor men have learned to better
At least say we,
When enticing regards ignite desire.

Fortunately neighbor Bob, stuck on TV,
Sits with his back to us
And cannot possibly see;
And just imagine the lady next door—
If she could possibly hear us—
Her frantic calls to the bomberos
Thus we carry on
In our third or thirteenth year
That neither age nor sickness can overtake
—as good as the postal service—
Our special deliveries
Whatever the inclemencies that break.

We do not need some Valentine signal
That newspapers print
And lit types favor
We have our own stalking pace
Of male bridging to female flavor
And nature's mastering fall.
Caught up in that universal
We bring to the world its own R & R
But only make it go farther.

Tuesdays

In the interest of espousal bliss
And something of a household dare
My wife and I
(You can tell the lead string here)
By the strictest of accords
Have set aside Tuesday
As a day of denial.
It's a calculated tease
By taking one step back
We make the heart grow fonder
And ever merrier Wednesday's release.
Like dieting at a colonic spa
We can anticipate the itch
Of a pending binge.

It's like a Lenten fast
Or for Sabbath we go slack
A new order of days
We commence on Tuesday.
Tuesday is a bright day
We all know its Mars' day
In the Romance tongues
And even in our plain speech
There lies compounded
The same martial thews and thighs
That left the Southern world confounded.

It's Monday that is bleak
When computers turn blue
No Lord died on Tuesday
It's Friday that is meatless
The day that we call "good,"
The day Jesus wears a hood.

We're beginning to misgive our day.
Eternal lamps don't sputter
All strong things hold to their ways
Without any diminution of days
Even Lysistrata went the full round
Not picking days and then sitting down
Vows without advisement
Are other than wise.
Thus admonishes Erasmus
And all his Reformation guys.

Let us now defer
In allotting our Sabbath
Postpone it to the hereafter
Where spirits hobnobbing
We can intermingle at will
And have no need to take our fill
Of respite or renewal
Spry among the contemplatives
Clean and clear
Like dancers leaping through the air
In meditative splendor sprung
And can smartly delay—
Days and names without number—
Thus turning all hours into one Tuesday.

Part Two
Other Poems

Rocks and Their Fellow Travelers

"Who, moving others are themselves as stone, unmoved ..."
(Quoted by Eva Brann, in *Homage to Americans*)

The graven testimony of sense
And the logics of difference
Should make any glossing clear
That nowhere in the catalogues of creation
Does it ever appear
That the Holy Spirit made Rocks and Boulders.
Precious stones, yes, when the rivers parted
But they were only indications of decline.

Rocks and such uncreated things
Were there before the beginning
And will still be there after the end.
Nothing like pathetic Gnostics
Who whip up contending Hierarchs
Rocks and boulders forfeit the game
They refuse the play
Indifference is their ready suit.
There is no prestige in the lowest depths
If lower depths fit them all the way.

They come from different worlds
No flourish of trumpets
To announce an approaching King
No generosity of spirit
Benevolence of imagination
Or a compassionate heart
Not even the simple contentment of the Lord
Who surveyed his early work
And found it good.
But drubbed by rocks and boulders
As paltry devices needing to be liked
Or a slavish eagerness to please

What thy want is just the opposite
Nothing but silence could them appease.

They have no truck even with God's opponents
In whom sentiment has come to uncover
Some tissues for elevation
My Esau about whom a friend wrote
That he was a hard man, a rock.
But he was the victim of a situation
Beguiled and doomed to drudgery
By a younger brother's skullduggery
Never-ending was his moan
About getting back his own.
And weary complaint about patrimony
Which did attract some sympathy
But not from those who live alone
And have no lineage to share
Unmoved and unmoving
Rocks and boulders laugh at what is fair.

Another was Luzbel, the Spanish Satan,
Who fell and fell again
At each relapse his legions grew thinner
Yielding finally to the odds of the winner.
Something boyish even childish
In his aspiration to rule and reign—
No one runs for President seven times
Is the lesson he never learned—
Comic even, like a Jack-in-the-box
But never a buffoon
Some scratch of redemption
In his need to aspire.
As the world goes,
If you add up and compare
The Scriptures are softies
Hardness of heart is mollified and rare.

Pagan classics tell a similar story.

That of Sisyphus
Stuck on the same track
Even the rocks come to deride
And watch him slip and slide
As he approaches the final divide
Believing once again
He will cross the line
Only to stumble
And dodge the rocks that tumble
Down the long mountain side,
Across the shore coming to rest
Wherever they abide
At the bottom of the silent sea.
Wondering what gets into this man
Who rolls his sleeves and girds his tunic
To try again
Only to lose his grip at the final footing.
How could he fail to understand
That after the pinnacle there is nothing to stay
But simply another downhill all the way?
With rocks there is only one outcome
Not even a big splash
No Romantic credit offered for trying
The creaking sound of bone against bone
Is the only sound from stone against stone.

These are fall-guys
Whose dithering brings some esteem
Then there are those who add to this theme.
Who become like rocks themselves
Closing their lives with a silence so resolute
So far from God but just as absolute
They deserve their own Rushmore
But rather than facings for all to see
They turn their bodies to the wall
Careless of when the ax lets fall.

Iago is the leader of this brigade

Against the melodrama of Italian rage
With Othello sending up such torments
To crash heaven's battlements
And break loose the falling "stones"
That would mitigate his pain
Or annihilate his brain.
But Iago seeks no such relief
So closed within himself
He knows where to find his end
"From this time forth I never will speak word."
No commendable story does he seek,
Such that would palliate his schemes
Not even death by fire-fed screams
But rather stones around his neck
And casting into the deep.
Where he will assume such a stance.
That even the fishes will poke and dart,
Unable to jostle him with a start.

It is only Lear who, as in so much more,
Knows the scandal in its highest sense.
They must have hearts of stone
Who do not howl at Cordelia's death,
Which takes away life's breath
And sends a crack down its middle
Creating a fissure that few can sustain.
Goneril bears her half of the bargain
Their society must endure
This lusting woman who killed her sister.
But cannot be faced down or brought to heel
"Do not ask me what I know,"
Are all the words her scorn intends
Such terseness brings to an end
Any outpourings of remorse,
Or brazen features of a dark renown
Do not lay your speeches on me
What I desire is the stillness at the bottom of the sea
Where no names are known,

No faces shown.

In Dante's infernal lower reaches
There are those who abandoned hope
Long times ago
Virgil trying to pry Bocca's story
Is told that he is out of his league.
Different tickets of transit are required
Not the soft soap of fame
But the hardness of heart
That would banish his name.
Dread silence of blank spaces
No desire, no response
Is adequate to the depths of those sunken faces.

Do you really believe
That Cain slew his brother
With the powdery jawbone of an ass?
Certainly a heavier stone was at hand
Especially the stones enrooted in the hearts of man.
Which for me explains Stonehenge.
They did not lug those ten-ton tocks
To tell the time, or the calendar of seasons
Nor were such ugly things
Suitable monuments to the majesty of kings.
In the roughness of their martial times
They needed twin pillars to express
The double strains in the make of humans.
Overtopping each is the cross-bar
Which serves as cap
Shutting off both desire and response.

God had no need to bring about rocks.
In the hollow chambers of the heart
There was ample space for humankind
To be left to their own concoctions.
Which not even divinity could restrain—
Evidence certain

That rocks and boulders were outside his range—
So free from its taint, he could not invent
The absolute silence of their chilled intent.

Huzzah for the kingdom of stone
And those who no longer aspire
Nor feel any need to atone.
You shall indeed be left alone
Free at last to gnarl your bone.

Wallet Poems IV

1.
TV fans the air waves
With fervent pleas or raves—
"Listen to me" is the constant holler
Like a drunk who has you by the collar—
Leaving a reservoir of mold
With no pitches left untold
All excited and no place to go
Giving new meanings to "shallow."
The only thing it brings together
Are 5-day plans for the weather.

When what the spirit requires
Is accumulations of thought
Refunding all that is store-bought
Or not self-taught
And brought to hold
Avoiding all that is canned,
Even quelling the tremors of hand.
A treasure hunt of expressive connection
Comes from books of mediated reflection.
Where what is ours puddles around
Until it ready is to be found.

2. A Dirge For Mary
Brimming with sexual pride
She flashed a big rock
"You didn't think I could get a man like that."
A nudge of flaunt we could have done without
But Mary was a novelist, whose heroines
Clawed and battled their ways
Up from the waterfronts of Seattle—
Mary's much-alikes.
Now in her sixties,
Her face cracked and creased

She fell into the sweep of his arms
The smiling bounty of his charms,
This handsome dancing man.
An expert in vibrating toys
And other more parlous ploys.
In months he sapped her savings
And at the last, her beneficiary,
Utilized his laboratory training
To stick with insulin her softer tissue
And take his profits from this woman without issue.

We were later to learn
That the police were on his trail
Waiting for one last kill—our Mary—
Before bringing him in.
Thus Mary, from Seattle's laden docks,
With her own literary skills
Was undone by a male vagrant
Who knew what opened the locks
To woman's long-losing love of love;
Some wild arousal
Almost a taunt
Committed her to places where predators haunt.

3. "Words, words, words"
   - Hamlet

(For Nelson and Stephanie)

Harvey Gross, the prime metricist of his day,
Whose approval expert poets sought,
At heart a composer
Who listened with lights dimmed
So that every note might be caught,
Lay at a hospice in Silver Springs
His body twisted and his mind in shreds
Yet feeling knighted by his book of verse
That Myron Simon and I worked to collect.

Suitably harmonious and precise
This son of the Moderns
Hailed them to every passing nurse.
Or hugged them nightly to his breast
Even when eating he would not let go.
With right hand he gouged slithery pasta
But with his left so guarded his hoard
That not a stain marred their keep,
Nor even giant strength could them wrest.

4.
A poem is drawn to its own completion
Fulfilling a selected pattern of design
But it also has a latent assignment
Working its way through the tunnels of mind.
How else explain its running insistence
And buzzing of a head crying for sleep,
Or phrases bestowed at morning's first light?

Thus Colombo found not the East
But Santo Domingo, waiting to be discovered,
A world that was there all the while,
Ready for its future to come swarming in.

Colombo's was a poetic disclosure;
The moving of each straight and sound
To a purpose they thought they found;
It was a program they never figured,
But certainly one their directions prefigured.

Dispatched

There, I've done it again
Is it the ingrained habit of the second son
The habit of silence
Withholding of response, or merely delay
That metastasizes into insuperable extent
Where any response is an embarrassment
Impossible to reverse or even indent?

Failure to respond to ally or friend
Even the carelessness of e-mail
Calls for a better explanation
Certainly it is not indifference
A faltering restraint
Nor sluggishness
Where all response is vain,
Nor a wall too high to climb
A simple cartolina, at the ready,
Is all it takes to erase the blame.

Is it a refusal to engage such putty?
Too easy to hasten a reply,
To rally the emotions
To a gregariousness of style?
I've done that often enough
One more time shouldn't be too tough.

Words aren't found wanting
Perhaps it's a sense of bonding
As if the friend were actually there
And didn't need a written record
But knew my reply by affinity's accord.

It's as if we were together in a car
Letting silence prevail
The journey is a long one
There's no need for words
Would the changing landscapes be lost
If we let it all subside?
Are words so important
Most of them redundant
To the binding that presides?

Yes, this is my apology,
A line of defense
Based on the settled nature
That what is will always be
And will not alter
No matter what is said
No packages or letters
Expedited through the air
Will change the meaning of having been there
We sit there forever,
Eternity's heir,
Time is our sediment and not a passing fair.

But some part of me wishes to add
That perhaps a word or two
Would temper the situation
And spare the humiliation
Of having lost our post in what is passing fair.

Profanities

Sitting on the patio deck
Working my then habitual cigar
Watching the zooming cars,
Escapees from the clogged freeways,
Converting streets into speedways,
But not polluting my auditory space
As I think of William Butler Yeats
And the municipal gallery he revisited.
From ballad and tale he knew them all
Those who presided over their times
And showed Ireland's history
In their bark-lined faces.
All coming to life once more in his rhymes.

What would he think of the partners of my youth,
Of Iggy appropriately classed as "ungraded,"
Who came to announce
Where we were fishing for minnies
That George Washington had just died.
This was April of '45;
But he was not far wrong.
For those wrenched by the Depression
As my Aunt Clara would say,
FDR was a savior
To the coal regions of Pennsylvania.

Then there was Ga-ga
Who adopted the stylish mode
Idling his passage along the streets—
Not many cars to hinder his ways—
Straddling a tin-can tied to a string,
Rhythm for the songs he tried to sing.
His brother Chicky was more refined,
As he demonstrated to us kids
How to blow up used rubbers
Through his thick shirt sleeve covers.

Profanities, nothing but profanities
The profanities of the profane.

Or the cowering Gypsy
Knocked clear across the hall
By Mr. Berlin, our principal,
Or his sister, to us kids in awe
Showed how high she could piss
Against St. John's church wall.
And the bug-eyed Jack
Who carried the Gypsy
Across the train tracks,
Where he had been foraging for copper
But found a live-wire instead
His fingers scorched together.
The same Jack who rallied
In Gmoie's favor—
Gmoie of Murder Inc. fame—
And received for his troubles
A State Trooper's club across his brain

Profanities, nothing but profanities
The profanities of the profane.

Or the golden one,
My hero and my star,
Who, as a sixth grader fought ninth-graders—
Can you imagine that? —
And won every game he pitched.
My mother gently came to tell me
That he was killed by the door-handle of a car
Where he was fishing by the canal
Which I still cannot understand
Funerals, o funerals, where we learned to kneel and pray
I bent to kiss his cold hand.

My heroes and my time
The figures go on.

After a winning game in Harrisburg
In which I made some demon shots
Stash conferred recognition
By kissing my head
The same Stash, whom years later,
Meeting disconsolate at a bar,
Told he was "on the bum."
I had no more tears to shed.

Profanities, nothing but profanities,
I would change it all, if I could.
Those things then obscure
Holding poisons without cure,
Profanities without name
We know now what to call them
Profanities of shame.

Ricardo Quinones is a scholar-critic, professor emeritus of Claremont McKenna College. He is the author of such prize-winning volumes as *The Changes of Cain: Violence and the Lost Brother in Cain-Abel Literature* (1991) and *Dualisms: The Agons of the Modern World* (2007), which was followed by *Erasmus and Voltaire: Why They Still Matter* (2010) and *North/South: The Great European Divide* (2016).

www.ingramcontent.com/pod-product-compliance
Lightning Source LLC
Chambersburg PA
CBHW050911300426
44111CB00010B/1481